2

Gnang Gnang - The delight.

Front cover
Detail from the *gong ageng* (Plate 2)

Plate 1
Kecher, height 11 in (28cm)

Sir Stamford Raffles
1781–1826
by G. F. Joseph ARA, 1817
By courtesy of
the Trustees of the
National Portrait
Gallery

Published by the Trustees of the British Museum London 1970

The Raffles Gamelan
A Historical Note

edited by William Fagg

with a biographical note
by Douglas Barrett

Errata

Plate 16 caption: for '*gamelau*' read '*gamelan*'
page 43   3rd paragraph 2nd line from end: delete 'not'
page 45   3rd paragraph 6th line: after 'spread' read 'wing'
page 58   2nd line: after 'between' read 'the'
Glossary: 3rd entry from bottom: for '*Pejnungging*' read '*Penjungging*'

Contents

Foreword

This 'historical note' does not pretend to cover – except in Raffles's own words – the musical aspects of the *gamelan*. This is an extremely complex subject – possibly the most complex in the whole field of ethnomusicology – and one on which we hope to arrange for some detailed research to be carried out in the next few months or years.

I am indebted to my friend Douglas Barrett, Keeper of Oriental Antiquities, for permission to reprint his admirable biographical note from the *British Museum Quarterly*, Volume XVIII (1953), pp 106–9. I have added two passages from Raffles's own writings: his brief account of music in Javanese culture from his Presidential Address to the Bataviaasch Genootschap van Kunsten en Wetenschappen on 24 April 1813, quoted from Lady Raffles's *Memoir*; and the longer and more detailed account of the *gamelan* in the *History of*

Java, 1817, the information in which we may suppose to have been checked with Raden Rana Dipura, whom he brought to England, and who stayed with him until he returned to the East. (It is odd, since this high-ranking Javanese apparently gave at least one performance – possibly on our *gamelan* – that Raffles's biographers, including his widow, make only the barest mention of his visit, and none of the importation of the *gamelan*.) Thanks are also due to the Trustees of the National Portrait Gallery, for permission to reproduce the Raffles portrait by G. F. Joseph ARA, and still more for agreeing to lend it to the exhibition. Miss Shelagh Weir, Assistant Keeper in the Department, has been in charge of the exhibition of the *gamelan*.

WILLIAM FAGG
Keeper of Ethnography

Plate 2
Gong ageng height 73½in (187cm)

Sir Thomas Stamford Raffles
by Douglas Barrett

In the extraordinary career of Thomas Stamford Raffles (1781–1826), his lieutenant-governorship of Java may seem but an apprenticeship to the last eight years of his short life. For it was only then that his restless energy, both as man of action and scholar, found permanent expression in the creation of Singapore and the establishment of the Royal Zoological Society. To Raffles himself his Javanese period must have been one of bitter disappointment. He came to Java in 1811 on the crest of the wave. Six years earlier he had been a clerk in Leadenhall Street. Now, but thirty years old, he was to be given a free hand in this rich island, the most important of the Dutch possessions in the East. He enjoyed the complete confidence of Lord Minto, the Governor-General of Bengal, and was equipped as none other to carry his plans into effect. Happily married, he was accompanied by his wife, a woman of great charm and character, and his dearest friend, John Leyden, one of the most gifted men who had ever come East. Five years later he was superseded in his command, and left the island in ill health and partial disgrace. His wife, Leyden, and Minto, were dead. It seemed that nothing of his work remained. But three achievements of enduring value survived his temporary fall – his approach to the peoples of the East, an example to all future administrators, his book *The History of Java*, and his collections.

In 1813 Raffles was unanimously elected president of the Bataviaasch Genootschap van Kunsten en Wetenschappen. This society, the earliest of its kind in the East, was founded in 1778 by the celebrated Rademacher. In the difficult period following his death it seems to have declined. It was Raffles's aim to revive its influence and to extend its scope to include archaeology and philology. His intention and its early results may best be seen in his Presidential Address and the papers which form the contents of the seventh volume of the *Verhandeling* of the Society. The enthusiasm of his assistants, both English and Dutch, was largely due to the famous Raffles charm. Though he habitually overworked, his smiling courtesy and composure never failed him. 'He spoke in smiles', said Abdullah, his Malay secretary. Thomas Horsfield, the distinguished American botanist and author of *Plantae Javanicae Rariores,* who had come to Java during the Dutch period, continued his work under the British régime. He combed the island for specimens, collecting at the same time bronzes for Raffles. He was perhaps not as well-beloved as Arnold and Jack, Raffles's botanists of the later Bencoolen days, nor fortunate enough to discover anything quite as exciting as the *Rafflesia Arnoldii*. Horsfield was later Keeper of the Indian Museum, Leadenhall Street, and thus conserved the very collections he had helped to assemble. These collections eventually came to the British Museum. Another assistant was John Crawfurd, who later was Raffles's second Resident at Singapore and whose *History of the Indian Archipelago* (1820) is one of the great early books on the subject. Crawfurd was interested in geology and the Museum possesses a collection of his rocks. But all Raffles's officers were expected to take an intelligent interest. There was Colonel Johnson, who discovered the temple ruins at Suku; Lieutenant Williams, who explored the Temples on Lawu Mountain; and John Lawrence, who collected bronzes in Kedu. The most devoted archaeologist was doubtless Colonel Colin Mackenzie. This serious sapper had already found time between campaigns and surveys to form an immense collection of material relating to Indian history and archaeology, and in 1797 he had discovered the most famous monument in the Deccan, the stupa at Amarāvatī. Though kept busy by Raffles as chairman of the land and revenue committee, he continued to indulge his hobby. He visited most of the archaeological sites in the island, and collected a mass of information, now in the Library of the Commonwealth Office – his papers contain an amusing archaeological catechism to which he subjected one of his Dutch colleagues – and several fine pieces of sculpture, now in the Indian Museum, Calcutta. The seventh volume of the *Verhandeling* of the Batavian Society, already mentioned, contains Mackenzie's account of his visit to the Prambanan group of temples, no doubt in the company of Newman, his draughtsman at Amarāvatī. Unfortunately we can only guess at the work which would have been accomplished by John Leyden, the most brilliant of Raffles's companions. This extraordinary polymath, best known through Lockhart's *Life of Scott,* died soon after the landing, having contracted fever while studying documents in a cold room at Batavia. The most important Dutch collector was Nicholas Engelhard, governor of the north-east coast from 1801 to 1808. He was the first European to take a systematic interest in Javanese art and many splendid pieces of sculpture, from Prambanan and Singasari, found their way into the garden of his house 'De Vrijheid' at Samarang. Many of these pieces are now in Leyden. Mention should also be made of the engineer-draughtsman, Cornelius, Wardenaar, van der Geugten, and Flikkenschild, many of whose drawings came into the possession of Raffles.

In most of this Raffles was the moving spirit. Of his own work during the little leisure his immense administrative duties allowed him, his book and collections are the best evidence. A keen linguist and zoologist, he had for some years steadily extended his knowledge of the East. Already a 'perfect Malay', he proceeded to make his own vocabulary of the languages of Java. His translation of the Brāta Yūdha, the national epic of Java, is still of the greatest interest. The translation was also given 'a poetical dress' by Raffles's cousin, the Rev Thomas Raffles, of Liverpool. He had for some years corresponded regularly with William Marsden, the doyen of Eastern studies and author of *The History of Sumatra* (1783). The best of his learned letters are to Marsden, himself a Malay scholar, having learned the language from the father of Abdullah, Raffles's secretary. 'I am collecting for you', Raffles writes in 1812, 'a variety of inscriptions found in different parts of Java. . . Drawings of all the ruined temples and images are in hand.' Several volumes of these drawings by the Dutch draughtsmen already mentioned and by Capt Baker are now in the Department of Oriental Antiquities. Some were engraved for the first and second editions of the *History of Java.* The remainder would, no doubt, have been used to illustrate the 'Antiquities of Java', a book advertised at the end of the *History,* but which Raffles never found the leisure to write. In 1813 he writes: 'The

Juliana takes home a very compact collection of quadrupeds, birds and insects, prepared by Dr Horsfield for the Oriental Museum at the India House. A large collection of dried plants is also sent.' No doubt the latter collection made its way to Soho Square – to Sir Joseph Banks and his librarian, the formidable Robert Brown, the first of Britain's botanists and the first Keeper of Botany in the British Museum. Wishing to see everything for himself, Raffles travelled extensively in the island, at great speed and through unexplored country, visiting, as he said, 'nearly all the remains of sculpture to be found'. He adds: 'Many of the Hindu deities have been found in small brass and copper casts: of these I have a collection containing nearly every deity in the Hindu mythology.' These bronzes, some 150 in number, and five pieces of sculpture are now in the Department of Oriental Antiquities. The collection came to the Museum in two portions. By far the larger was presented in 1859 by the Rev Raffles Flint, the executor of the second Lady Raffles, and the son of Raffles's favourite sister, Mary Ann. The second portion was given in 1939 by Mrs Drake, granddaughter of Raffles Flint. It included a number of Javanese bronzes, including one of superb quality, and several eighteenth-century Burmese figures. Raffles seems to have been particularly fond of this part of his collection, if we may judge from G. F. Joseph's portrait, painted soon after Raffles's return to England from Java. It was presented to the National Portrait Gallery in 1859 by the Rev Raffles Flint (frontispiece). On his table stand a fine figure of the Singasari period and one of the most beautiful of his bronzes. It is a pity that neither piece

was closely observed by the artist, his conception of the Singasari figure bearing as much resemblance to the original as the Rev Thomas Raffles's poetical version of the Brāta Yūdha to the Javanese epic. Thanks to Raffles the British Museum possesses the finest collection of Javanese sculpture outside Java and Holland. Nor is this all. In the Department of Ethnography are Raffles's *Gamelan*, the complete band of instruments, his large collection of weapons, his *Topeng* masks, his puppets and hide *Wayang* figures. There are probably no *Wayang* figures, even in Java, earlier than Raffles's. There are certainly none finer in quality. Examples of all these objects are illustrated in Raffles's book, which remained supreme in this field until the work of the great Dutch scholars at the end of the nineteenth century. Though superseded in detail, it still retains, more than any other book, the atmosphere and feel of his beloved island.

Most of Raffles's collections from the Java period survive, either in the British Museum, at Bloomsbury and South Kensington, or at Kew. The story of the loss of the collections formed during his second period in the East at Bencoolen and Singapore, indicates Raffles's quality, as man and collector. Though much had been sent home, he kept the best things by him until that day in 1823 when having decided to leave the East for ever, he ordered Abdullah to pack his collections in their hundreds of boxes – manuscripts, books, paintings, sculpture, animals, birds, flowers, insects, shells, and rocks. 'On all these', said Abdullah, 'he placed a value greater than gold.' From Singapore Raffles sailed to Bencoolen, where the rest of his collection was packed.

Plate 3
Detail from the *gong ageng*

At dawn on 2 February 1824, he sailed for home on the
Fame. That same evening the ship caught fire; the
passengers took to the boats and the collections were
left to burn. By 2 o'clock the next day, Raffles was back
at Bencoolen. Dangerously ill, he slept for fifteen hours,
then set his draughtsmen and hunters to work to make
new drawings and to procure fresh specimens. He
himself began to draw a new map of Sumatra.

The Raffles Gamelan
by William Fagg

Another great English proconsul had preceded Raffles by some 235 years in reporting on the music of the *gamelan*, though Raffles was probably unaware of the fact. As Jaap Kunst notes (in *Music in Java*, 1949): 'The oldest European record of Javanese music is found in the logbook of Sir Francis Drake, who, in the course of his famous voyage round the world in *The Golden Hind* in 1580, visited the South coast of Java; he first gave a performance with his own musicians in honour of "Raia Donan, King of Java" and afterwards heard "his country-musick, which though it were of a very strange kind, yet the sound was pleasant and delightfull".' However, Raffles was certainly the first Englishman, and probably also the first European, to think of bringing home a whole orchestra, and not merely one orchestra but two. For although the British Museum specimen is by far the better-known, there is a second *gamelan*, of a different type, at Claydon House, the seat of the Verney family, at Bletchley in Buckinghamshire. The house is now a National Trust property, but the *gamelan* is on loan from the family for exhibition there.

Some comparative research was begun on the two sets some years ago, which it is now hoped to carry forward and complete in the near future. There is some reason to suspect that, at some time before 1859 (when the British Museum received its *gamelan*), some of the metallophone keys may have been inadvertently transposed between the two sets. This would no doubt have happened after the departure from England in 1820 of Raden Rana Dipura, the Javanese chief who came here with Raffles in 1816 and who appears to have been an accomplished musician (Plate 4). The Claydon House set is not the one described by Raffles in *The History of Java*, 1817 (Plate 7), and he nowhere mentions that he had collected any examples. By the same token, we have no evidence as to the part of Java from which either orchestra came, although the quality of the carving is so high and the gilding so lavish in the Museum set that it is likely to have belonged to the ruler of one of the royal courts (*kraton*). In the courts the orchestras were treated with great care, often having a special storeroom set aside for them, and this would account for the generally good condition of the instruments today. There is no way of knowing how old the orchestra was when Raffles acquired it.

Gamelan had, and still have, an important place in the cultural life of the Javanese people. There were various kinds of *gamelan*, the main differences between them being in the instruments making up each orchestra and the tonal system employed. The orchestras could also contain from a few instruments to more than thirty. Orchestras of different sizes and containing various combinations of instruments are traditionally an essential accompaniment to puppet shows, dance-dramas, feasts and ceremonies. In the performances of the shadow puppets (*wayang kulit* or *wayang purwa*), the orchestra highlights and accentuates the moments of drama, and music appropriate to the personality of the various main characters accompanies their appearance on the screen.

Detailed information on Javanese music can be obtained from Jaap Kunst, *Music in Java*, The Hague, 1949, and Mantle Hood, *Patet in Javanese Music*, Groningen, 1954.

Together with the *gamelan*, the British Museum acquired from the family in 1859 a large number of Javanese puppets and masks, and also a number of antiquities (which are in the Department of Oriental Antiquities). The puppets are the subject of a booklet by Jeune Scott-Kemball, which relates to the exhibition in an adjoining room.

Plate 4
Portrait drawing of the Javanese chief, Raden Rana Dipura, who came to Britain with Raffles in 1816 and returned with him to the East in 1820. From *The History of Java*, 1817

Plate 5
Bonang length 71in (181cm)
Plate 6
Detail from the *bonang*

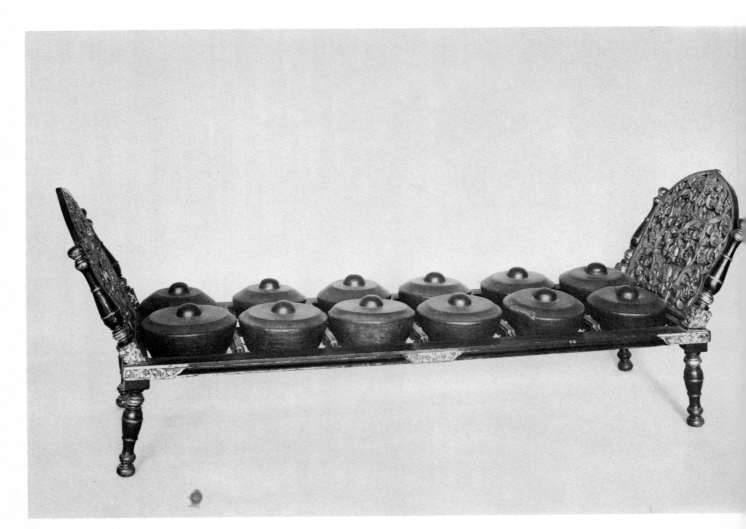

Raffles on Javanese Music I

From a Discourse delivered at a Meeting of the Society of Arts and Sciences, in Batavia, on the Twenty-fourth day of April, 1813, being the Anniversary of the Institution. By the Hon THOMAS STAMFORD RAFFLES, President.

There are in use for ordinary and popular compositions five different kinds of regular measured stanzas, termed *Tembang,* adapted to the subject treated of, whether heroic, amorous, or otherwise; these are termed *Asmoron Dono, Dandang Gula, Sinom, Durmo,* and *Pangkur.* In the higher compositions, and particularly in the Kawi, these measures are still more varied, and in number upwards of twenty, twelve of which correspond in name with the stanzas used in the poetry of continental India.

In repeating these compositions, they are chaunted, or rather drawled out in regular metre according to rules laid down for the long and short syllables. Dramatic representations of various kinds form the constant recreation of the higher classes of society, and the most polished amusement of the country; these consist of the *Wayang Kulit* or Scenic Shadows, in which the several heroes of the Drama, represented in a diminutive size, are made to perform their entrances and their exits behind a transparent curtain; the subjects of these representations are taken either from the more ancient works of the B'rata Yud'ha or Romo, and then denominated *Wayang Purwo,* or from the history of *Panji,* the most renowned hero of Java story, and then termed *Wayang Gedog.* The *Wayang Wong,* in which men personify the heroes of the B'rata Yud'ha and Romo is also termed *Wayang Purwo;* they have also the *Topeng,* in which men, wearing masks, personify those immortalised in the history of Panji, and the *Wayang Klitic* or *Koritchil,* not unlike a puppet-show in Europe, in which diminutive wooden figures personify the heroes of Majapahit.

These dramatic exhibitions are accompanied by performances on the Gamelan, or musical instruments of the Javanese, of which there are several distinct sets; the *Salindro,* which accompanies the performances from the B'rata Yud'ha and Romo, as well as the Topeng; the *Pelog* which accompanies the Wayang Gedog, the *Kodok Ngokek, Chara Bali, Senenan* and others; the Javanese music is peculiarly harmonious, but the gamut is imperfect.

Plate 7
The instruments of a *gamelan* (probably drawn from an orchestra in Java). From *The History of Java,* 1817

Musical Instruments
Gamelan Salindro

1	Gambang Gangsa.	5	Saron.	9	Gong.	14	Kendang.
2	Gambang Kayu.	6	Demong.	10	Kenong.	15	Chelempung.
3	Bonang or Kromo.	7	Selantam.	11	Ketuk.	16	Suling.
4	Gender.	8	Kecher.	12	Kumpul.	17	Rebab.
				13	Ketipung.		

London Published by Black, Parbury & Allen, Leadenhall Street 1817.

Raffles on Javanese Music II

From *The History of Java*, 2 volumes, London 1817, Volume I pp 469–72.

The musical instruments of the Javans are peculiar. Several of them are necessary to compose a *gámelan*, set, or band: of these there are several varieties. The *gámelan salíndro*, which is the most perfect, consists of the several instruments represented in the plate [Plate 7]. In the *gámelan pélog*, the instruments are much larger and louder; the *bónang* or *krómo*, has sometimes only ten, and sometimes as many as fourteen notes. Both of these *gámelans* are employed as accompaniments to the *wáyangs*. The *gámelan míring* partakes of the two former, and is employed to accompany the *wáyang klítik*. In the *gámelan múng'gang*, called also *kódok ng'órek*, from its resembling the croaking of frogs, the *bónang* has fifteen notes, and the *kécher* resembles the triangle: neither the *génder*, *salentam*, *sarón*, nor *chalémpung* are included in this set; this *gámelan* is considered the most ancient, and is played at tournaments, in processions, etc. In the *chára báli*, or *chára wángsul*, the *rebáb*, or viol, is not used: in other respects the instruments are the same as in the *salíndro*, except that they are as large as in the *pélog*. The *gámelan sekáten*, which resembles the *pélog*, except that the instruments are still larger and louder, is restricted to the use of the sovereign, and seldom played, except on great occasions, as during eight days of the festival of *Múlut*. The *gámelan srúnen* is used in processions of state and in war, being properly the martial music of the country, in which, besides the ordinary instruments, a particular *gong* and trumpets are introduced.

The plate will afford a better idea of the form of these instruments than any verbal description. Most of them resemble the *staccáto* or harmonica, and the sound is produced by the stroke of a hammer. The *gámbang káyu* has wooden plates, sixteen or seventeen in number: the *gámbang gángsa*, of which there are several in each band, has metal plates.

In the *génder* the metal plates are thin, of a different form, and suspended by strings. The *gong*, represented (No 9) in the plate, is usually three feet in diameter. The *bónang*, *kénong*, and *ketók*, are of metal, and are suspended by tightened cords to favour the vibration. The *kécher*, shewn in the plate, corresponds with the cymbal. The hammers with which the larger instruments are struck are either wound round at the end with cloth, or the elastic gum, in order to soften the sound. The drum is struck with the open hand and fingers only. The *chalémpung* is a stringed instrument, with from ten to fifteen wires, which are sounded with the finger, after the manner of the harp.

The person who leads the band performs upon the *rebáb* (No 17), an instrument which, having a neck, and two strings pitched by pegs, is capable of producing perfect intonation and a variety of sounds, by shortening the strings with the pressure of the finger.

The *gámbang káyu* (No 2) is a kind of *staccáto*, consisting of wooden bars of graduated lengths, placed across a kind of boat, which, when skilfully struck with a sort of mallet, produce pleasing tones, either grave or acute. The lowest and highest sounds of the instrument differ from each other by the interval of three octaves and a major third: the intermediate sounds of each octave from the lowest note are a second, third, fifth, and sixth.

Plate 8
Kenong height 27½in (70cm)

23

Plate 9
Detail from the *kenong*

This instrument is general throughout the Archipelago, and is frequently played alone, or accompanied only by the drum and a small *gong*. *Ráden Rána Dipúra*, a native of Java, who accompanied me to England, played on this instrument several of his national melodies before an eminent composer, all of which were found to bear a strong resemblance to the oldest music of Scotland, the distinctive character of both, as well as of Indian music in general, being determined by the want of the fourth and seventh of the key and of all the semitones.[1] By reiteration several of the sounds are artfully prolonged much beyond their noted length, which produces an irregularity of measure that might both perplex and offend the educated ear of an accompanying timeist. The rhythm of the sections (from extension and contraction) appears very imperfect.

The *bónang* or *krómo* (No 3), the *sáron* (No 5), the *démong* (No 6), and *selántam* (No 7), are *staccátos* of metallic bars, and a sort of bells placed on a frame. They contain a regular diatonic scale, and nearly two octaves. These, however, are never played singly, but harmonise with the instrument on which the air is played.

The *gongs* (No 9) are perhaps the noblest instruments of the kind that have been brought to Europe: I am assured that they are very superior to that which was admitted in the terrific scenes of the serious ballet representing the death of Captain Cook. Suspended in frames, and struck by a mallet covered with cloth or elastic gum, they sustain the harmonious triad in a very perfect manner, and are probably the most powerful

and musical of all monotonous instruments. They might be introduced with advantage in lieu of large drums. They have the advantage of being melifluous, and capable of accompanying pathetic strains. The two *gongs* differ from each other by one note.

The above observations apply particularly to the *gámelan pélog*, which usually accompanies the recitation of the popular poems of the country. The *gámbang káyu* of the *salíndru* appears only to differ in being in another key, which is considered better suited to the occasions in which that kind of *gámelan* is used.

The airs which are exhibited in the plate [endpaper] are selected from several written down by a gentleman at *Semárang,* as they were played on the *rebáb* of the *gámelan pélog,* and may afford a further illustration of the nature of their music.

But it is the harmony and pleasing sound of all the instruments united, which gives the music of Java its peculiar character among Asiatics. The sounds produced on several of the instruments are peculiarly rich, and when heard at a distance have been frequently compared to those produced on the harmonic glasses. The airs, however simple and monotonous they may appear of themselves, when played on the *gámbang káyu,* or accompanied by the other instruments, never tire on the ear, and it is not unusual for the *gámelan* to play for many days and nights in succession.

The Javans do not note down or commit their music to writing: the national airs, of which I have myself counted above a hundred, are preserved by the ear alone. Those which are exhibited in the plate are among the most popular: but there are a variety which

[1] The same observation has, I believe, been made on the character of the Grecian music.

Plate 10 right
Saron (instrument with metal keys)
length 58in (147cm)
Plate 11 below
Saron demong (instrument with metal keys)
length 39½in (100cm)

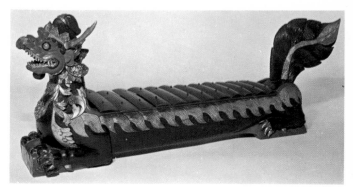

Plate 12
Gender (instrument with metal keys)
length 48½in (123cm)

Plate 13
Gambang kayu (instrument with wooden
keys) length 58in (147cm)

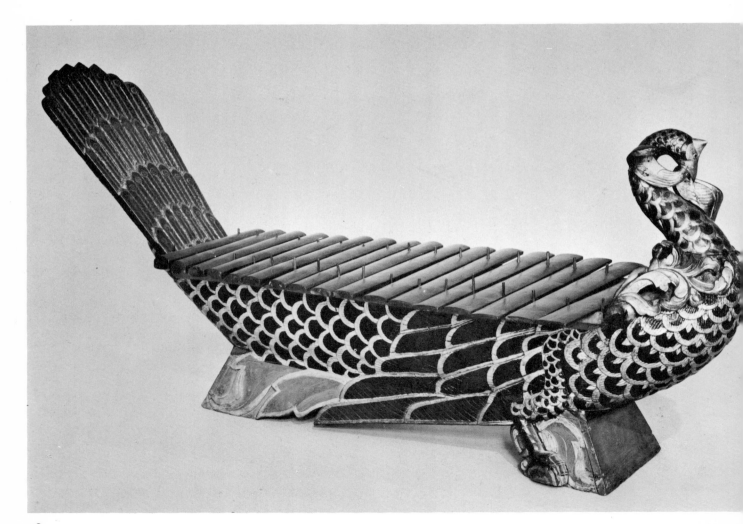

Plate 14
Ketipung length 16in (41cm)

are played on occasions of rejoicing and festivity, which it would be difficult to note down; if, indeed, they can be called airs at all, the sounds produced rather resembling the chiming of bells than a melody. Thus, when a great man arrives at the native seat of government, the tune of *kébu gíru,* 'buffaloes frisking', is played, and a variety of others of the same nature, which diffuse the same kind of joy and gaiety among all assembled, as the quick ringing of bells in the churches of England.

A complete set of the *gámelan pélog* costs from a thousand to six hundred dollars (£250 to £400), but second-hand sets are frequently disposed of. The principal manufacture is at *Grésik,* and the *gongs* in particular furnish a valuable article of export. Every native chief in authority has one or more *gámelans,* and there are more or less perfect sets in all the populous towns of the eastern provinces.

In some of the interior, and in particular in the *Súnda* districts, the inhabitants still perform on a rude instrument of *bámbu,* called the *ángklung,* of which a representation is given in one of [Raffles's] plates. This instrument is formed of five or more tubes of *bámbu,* cut at the end after the manner of the barrels of an organ. These, which are of graduated lengths, from about twenty to eight inches, are placed in a frame, in such a manner as to move to a certain extent from their position, and to vibrate on the frame being shaken. A troop of from ten to fifty mountaineers, each with an *ángklung,* and accompanied by one or two others with a small drum played with the open hand, always perform upon this instrument on occasions of festivity in the

29

Plate 15
Kendang length 28in (71cm)

Súnda districts. The upper part of the instrument, and the parties themselves, are generally decorated with common feathers, and the performers, in their appearance and action, are frequently as grotesque and wild as can be imagined. There is something, however, so extremely simple, and at the same time gay, in the sound produced by the rattling of these *bámbu* tubes, that I confess I have never heard the *ángklung* without pleasure. The Javans say the first music of which they have an idea was produced by the accidental admission of the air into a *bámbu* tube, which was left hanging on a tree, and that the *ángklung* was the first improvement upon this Eolian music. With regard to the music of the *gámelan,* 'that', they say, 'was procured from heaven, and we have a long story about it'.

A wind instrument, of the nature of a flute, but in length some feet, with a proportionate diameter, is sometimes introduced in the *gámelans;* but this is not usual in Java, though in *Báli* it is general.

The *trawángsa* is a stringed instrument, not very unlike a guitar, which is occasionally found in the *Súnda* districts: it is by no means general. I recollect to have once heard an old blind bard at *Chiánjur* play upon this instrument, reciting at the same time traditions respecting *Pajajáran,* and the ancient history of the country, which had probably never been committed to writing.

Plate 16
Old style *gamelan* of a Sundanese Regent.
Photograph: Royal Tropical Institute,
Amsterdam